T0147190

Caley's
GOAL

JUDY SELK SEAL

authorHOUSE®

AuthorHouse™
1663 Liberty Drive
Bloomington, IN 47403
www.authorhouse.com
Phone: 1 (800) 839-8640

Published by AuthorHouse 06/25/2019

ISBN: 978-1-7283-1040-4 (sc)
ISBN: 978-1-7283-1038-1 (hc)
ISBN: 978-1-7283-1039-8 (e)

Library of Congress Control Number: 2019906149

Print information available on the last page.

For my grandchildren,
always an inspiration to me.
For Cammi Granato, the captain of the women's hockey team
that won gold medals in the Nagano, Japan,
and Salt Lake City Olympics—
and for Caley's mother and all mothers who drive through
snowstorms so their daughters can play hockey.

CHAPTER 1

My head keeps going up and down, back and forth, like a bobblehead doll. *Clink, thunk, swish*—the pucks keep coming across the ice. I'm stopping some; others never even reach the net. And then there are those that shoot right past me.

All over the ice, kids are practicing. Some skate around cones. Others skate backward and run into everyone. The Rangers, my teammates, are lined up with piles of pucks they keep shooting at me. And I'm stuck in this stupid net.

In Detroit it seems nearly everyone plays hockey. There are after-school recreational leagues, like our Beginners Eleven and Under League, all over town. In our family, both of my brothers are in a league, and our dad plays for the Detroit Redwings. So here I am playing hockey too. I love it—but not goaltending.

Finally, a whistle blows. The pucks stop. Hockey practice is over.

"Good job, Caley," says Coach. "You're becoming a good goaltender."

Thanks, I think. *Do I really want to be a good goaltender?*

"Now, listen up, girls. Remember we have a game tomorrow night at six o'clock. Be there in your gear and on the ice. Everyone, remember to bring all of your equipment—no leaving some of it at home. Caley will be our goaltender for the night."

I roll my eyes and sigh, thinking, *Why am I always the goalie? We're supposed to change positions. I hate being the goalie all the time.*

"That was a fun drill," says Alex, her dark eyes flashing. "We got a lot of chances to hit the puck into the net." With a grin, she gives her long black hair a toss and does her famous thumbs-up as we skate off the rink in our old practice jerseys.

Alex gives that thumbs-up everywhere for everything to everybody. We tease her at school. It gets lots of attention, and I guess that's why she does it.

She adds, "That drill was more fun than skating backward and forward around those yellow cone things the coach puts on the ice for practice. Remember the awful drills we did last year?"

We head for the locker room, trying to avoid those kids skating backward, who haven't given up. The room smells like sweat and wet coats. It's cold and ugly. Benches are nailed to every wall; gear is thrown everywhere. We get pushed around in a steady stream of kids coming and going.

Suddenly, the smallest girl on the team is standing in front of me. She isn't much more than half the size of Madison, the oldest and biggest girl on the team. She has long, curly brown hair, a big helmet, and a loud voice.

"Ha!" the voice shouts. "You're going to be the goaltender again. I'm always a forward. I score the most goals. The team can't get along without me. They need me. All you do is stand around in the net. Do you think you're important—because of your dad?"

"Nope, thank you very much. What's your problem?" I say.

The back of her helmet marches away like a head with legs. I feel my face getting warm and scrunching up into *the look*. I take a deep breath.

"Alex, who is that?"

"Don't you know Emily?"

I don't know her, and I don't need her giving me a hard time about being the goalie. I'm mad.

"You know how much I love to play hockey, Alex," I say, pulling on my knitted cap. I find my coat and boots and pack up my gear.

She shrugs and says, "Of course you like to play hockey. Your whole family plays hockey. Well, not your mother." Alex looks at me strangely. "What's your problem? Why are you being so weird? Do you want to tell me anything else I already know? What are you going to do besides whine?"

"I'm not whining. I don't know if I can do anything. The coach makes those decisions, and he seems stuck on my being the goalie. He can be a little weird sometimes."

"I know. He yells a lot and keeps saying 'Have fun' after one of his attacks."

I roll my eyes to show how dumb I think that is and say, "Let's go. My mom's waiting."

I sigh as I hurry out of the rink. Figuring out the rest of my life will have to wait at least until tomorrow.

I hunch my shoulders and bend my head down against the wind and snow. I see Mom is already next to the curb, the motor running. I hope the car is warm.

"See you at school," Alex calls as she climbs into her family's van. I'm so busy sulking that I forget to say goodbye.

As I get in my mom's car, I think about things.

My dad thinks girl goaltenders are cool, and he wants me to be one. I want him to be proud of me. What would he say if he knew I didn't like it? I should like it. What's wrong with me? I guess taking my turn now and then is okay. That's fair.

CHAPTER 2

Tonight at the rink, we're fired up. There are high fives and shouts of "Yeah, Rangers!" and "What a team!" We're talking all the time. Being on a real hockey team is new and exciting. I love the feeling of the air on my face as I race up and down the ice while warming up. I love picking up a stray puck, taking it down the ice, and shooting it. The most fun of all is hitting the puck into the net—even if it's not a game.

Coach is yelling, "Gather 'round and listen up. Take your positions—first string on the ice, Caley in the net, the rest of you on the bench. Let's go. Remember what I told you. Stay in position. Keep your eye on the puck. Focus! You can beat this team."

The Rangers gather on the ice. I head for the net, sighing as I get into position. The whistle blows. They drop the puck. The game is starting. I'm ready.

Crouching in my net, I mumble, "Keep your eye on the puck. Focus."

My team scrambles in the middle of the rink. The puck bounces everywhere. It swishes out all over the ice. No one hits hard. Players trip and fall on each other.

The minutes tick down. The play is still on the other end of the ice. Suddenly, a small player breaks away. It's Emily. She carries the puck down the ice and flips it right into the net.

Score!

My teammates hug and cheer, celebrating on the other end of the ice. They can't hear me cheer. I hug my water bottle. I want to be with my team.

The whistle blows and play resumes. I crouch in my net. We score again, and then the period ends with a score of two to zero. The other team never got to my end of the ice.

What defense our team has. They're fired up.

The next period starts, and I feel bored, stupid, depressed, and grumpy.

There's still a lot of colliding and milling around on the ice. By the middle of the second period, we finally get it together.

Emily flips the puck to Alex. She fires it in. She scores.

"Good shot, Alex," I yell. She can't hear me.

The period ends with a score of three to zero. Our defense has kept the other team on their end of the ice for another whole period. It's embarrassing.

I wish I had my iPod. I bet coach would love that. Ha.

The third period goes the same way as the first and second. My team scores twice. The puck stays on the other end of the ice. We win five to zero.

"Good job, girls," says Coach.

"Some game," says Alex as we skate off the ice to the locker room. Everyone laughs, talks, and gives each other high fives.

"They were an easy team to beat, but we're shaping up as a good team," I say.

"So," Alex says. "What's your problem? You look grumpy."

"It's boring."

"We all take turns being goalie," she says. "We're learning all the positions."

"I'm doing it more than everybody else."

"That's because you're better at it." She gives me a sly grin.

"Duh, then I shouldn't have to be the goalie so often. I'll bet someone else on the team would like to do it for a change. They'd be good too. We're all supposed to be learning."

"You know, you won't have to be a goaltender for the rest of your life. I mean, you're only eleven, just like me."

"My whole life—how depressing. I'll have to do something. Think of all the goals I could score if I just didn't have to be the dumb goalie all the time, stuck in that stupid net," I say.

She laughs so hard that she can hardly talk.

"So what're you going to do?" she says, finally recovering. "About your hockey career and the rest of your life?"

"Just keep laughing, Alex. I don't know if I can do anything. The coach makes those decisions."

"I know. But he changes his mind a lot. He's always moving players around," Alex says.

"Except when it comes to me," I say, grumbling.

"Well, I have four pages of math to do tonight before I go to bed." Alex sighs as we're leaving the rink. "I'd better hurry. Figuring out the rest of your life will have to wait at least until tomorrow."

"You're right—enough for tonight."

We both giggle as we leave the locker room. She's my best friend, and we're good at giggling.

My mom is in the crowded lobby. She's on the other side of it with my little sister, Tara, talking to some parents. Tara is playing video games on the quarter machines. She catches sight of me and runs over.

"Do you have any quarters, Caley? There are none left in the whole building."

That includes me.

We work our way over to Mom, lugging the big hockey bag.

"Be careful, Tara. If we run into anyone, we'll knock them over."

It's noisy, hot, and smelly. There are kids pushing and shoving everywhere. Besides wet coats and mittens, there's old food smells, like popcorn and hot dogs. I love it.

In the car I think about what to do to become a forward. "How do I get out of being the goaltender?"

"What are you muttering about?" Mom asks as we're driving home.

"I'm not muttering."

"Yes, you are. Plus, you're staring into space and sighing and fidgeting."

"Just trying to figure something out."

"Can I help?"

"Not yet, Mom, I'm still thinking."

"Yes, I can see that." She grins.

CHAPTER 3

In class the next day, we discuss the history of Native American tribes along the Carolina coast when the Spanish invaded. Most tribes were slaughtered or died of diseases the Spanish brought. One group just disappeared. Some historians believe they hid out until the Spaniards left, and then they survived. They took action and saved themselves.

Is that the answer to my goalie problem? I think. *Simple. If it worked for the early people, maybe it will work for me. I need to take action to save myself—or quit complaining.*

I spot Alex at our favorite table in the cafeteria. I can't wait to tell her what I figured out. We're having ham sandwiches and chopped up apples, my favorite school lunch. I sit down, and we talk about hockey.

"Alex, you want to hear my idea?"

"Not another idea. Which one are you thinking about now?"

"Do you think if I asked Coach, he would let me be a forward instead of the goaltender?"

"Sure, so what's the big deal?" She coughs on apples." Why do you think it's so hard?"

"What if he says no or thinks I'm asking for special treatment? Maybe he'll get irritated and make me sit on the bench all the time. Maybe he'll say being a goalie is good for me. You know how adults always say that."

"You've been goaltending a lot, so maybe he'll let you change positions," Alex says.

"Hey, you could tell Coach you want to be goaltender for a change?" I ask, sneaking a look at her.

"No way," she says. "Nice try."

"What if I'm a bad goalie? He'd pull me out of the game. That might work."

"You're too good at goaltending and too competitive to pretend you're awful."

"So I'm back to talking to Coach. Maybe he won't think I'm asking for special treatment, if I say it the right way."

"Ask your dad. He plays professional hockey. He knows everything."

"Dad's the special treatment I'm worried about. Besides, he'll just say if you want something, go for it. He always says that," I say.

"Why don't you ask your dad to talk to Coach? That's easy."

"I need to do this myself."

"So, there's your answer. Go for it. Besides it's the only way Coach will know how you feel," Alex says, reassuring me.

"Practice isn't until next week. I'll have to wait and think."

"Maybe you'll start to like it if you keep trying."

I roll my eyes at her and unwrap a chocolate cupcake that I'd hidden in my knapsack this morning, before my brothers got it. There's nothing like a chocolate cupcake with white frosting to help me think. I need to think.

The goalie thing hangs over my head during my saxophone lesson, and it still hangs over my head at my play rehearsal on Saturday morning. I only have a few lines, so most of the time I stand around and worry about how to get out of goaltending.

What if he says no? I will really be stuck. I'll never score goals. Or what

if he yells a lot and makes me feel awful? I can handle that if he says yes. I wish I knew Coach better.

Dad helps with practice sometimes and says he could never coach beginners like us. He wouldn't be able to teach the game at this basic level. We must be hard work. I can tell Coach tries to be extra nice so nobody starts crying—not me, of course, but somebody might.

I'm so worried and scared that I wonder if maybe I should just suck it up and be a goalie.

Before I know it, it's next week. Alex and I are in the locker room before practice when she says, "So have you decided what to do with the rest of your life and hockey career, Caley?" She can hardly control her giggles. She's not being serious.

"I know what I'm going to do. I've made up my mind. You're right; if I don't speak up, I could be a goalie forever—crouching in that little net, all by myself, while people shoot pucks at me. You know how they always blame the goalie when the team loses. I mean, in general, not our team. We never lose."

"I knew you'd talk to him. And you'll be a forward in the next game, score lots of goals."

"I'll have to find a good time to ask him. You know how it is when you try to talk to adults, like teachers, coaches, and mothers. If they're busy, they don't always pay attention."

"You've got that right. We have lots of kids in our family. Getting noticed can be tricky," Alex says.

"I'll practice what to say and say it fast. I need to get it all out before he loses interest or starts to yell or I get too scared and throw up," I say.

Practice moves along, and I feel I am doing everything wrong. I feel like I am going to throw up. My hands are sweaty. I can hear myself blowing air out in big sighs, and I hope no one hears me.

Why is it so hard to talk to adults in charge of things? I guess because I never know how they think or what they will do or say. Will he say I should know my place? All he can say is yes or no. So why am I so scared?

My hands are sweaty, and so is my hair.

What will Dad say when he finds out I asked to play forward instead of goalie? He'll want a good reason. I hope he's not disappointed in me. He really wants me to be a goalie. I'm such a worrier.

I keep looking for the right time to talk to Coach. It's hard with all the pucks coming at me. He always seems busy with setting up drills, organizing his helpers, and shouting instructions.

Finally, drills are over, and he's alone with his clipboard. He's a small man and always wears the same brown jacket. His hair is cut really short; I think it's so no one will notice he's getting bald. Glancing at Alex I say, "This is it!"

She gives her thumbs-up.

I let out a big breath and slowly skate over to Coach. I just stand there. My mouth feels stuck. Finally, a sound comes out.

"Excuse me, Coach. Excuse me. Um, can I ask you something?" I say.

"What?" He doesn't look up.

"I've been the goaltender a lot lately. Do you think maybe I can play offense in the next game? I might even score a goal."

"You don't like being the goalie?" he asks, finally taking a look at me. "But you're good at it. What's wrong with being a goalie? It's the most important position on the team."

"No," I say, firmly. He looks at me for a minute, as if he's thinking. He seems irritated. His eyes are mad.

"You're a big help to the team in that position," he says. "Did your dad put you up to this?"

He doesn't wait for an answer. He slams the clipboard down against his side and lets out a big sigh.

All he says is, "Don't forget to bring the goaltending equipment with you for your replacement. Remember, we pass it around because it's expensive."

"I will. Thanks!" What a relief. It's done. He didn't even yell, but I can tell he's not happy.

Now all I have to do is prove I can be a good forward.

CHAPTER 4

Down in my basement, I put on my roller blades, and I'm ready to go. I pick up a hockey stick and skate around, collecting pucks. I put them at different distances from the net down at the far end. Skating I hit one after another from different angles into the net.

"Why are you whacking pucks all over the place? I can hear you upstairs," says my brother Dean, grinning.

"Coach says I can be a forward next week, not a goalie. I want to be good and score a goal."

"I can see you need help—lots of help. I'll show you some moves."

"I heard Dad say you were a stick handler with good hands. You're a good teacher too."

"Just keep practicing. I'll help this week when I have time," Dean says.

"Dean, with your help, I might even score in the next game. If I'm not a good forward, Coach might make me be a goalie again."

"So what's wrong with being the goalie?"

"I don't like it. I'd rather be skating and shooting with my team, up and down the ice. You're a left winger. Why aren't you ever the goalie?" I ask.

Laughing, he says, "I'd rather be skating and shooting with my team."

"See."

"If you don't want to be a goalie, Caley, stop talking and start hitting some pucks at the net," he orders. "Maybe you'll get one in." He laughs again. I really love him.

I practice every day after school until Saturday, the day I'll be a forward. Sometimes my brother Jake comes downstairs and grins.

"You don't really think you're going to score the first time you play offense, do you?"

I give him a look and try to make it ferocious. Jake isn't impressed. He always gives me a hard time. He thinks he's funny.

CHAPTER 5

Finally, it's Saturday. It's exciting to pack my faded, old hockey bag, a big brother hand-me-down. My grandma watches as in goes my red and blue Rangers uniform, followed by my skates, socks, helmet, gloves, shin pads, elbow pads, and finally the goalie face mask and chest protector.

"That's a lot of equipment. Why don't you let one of your brothers help you?" asks Grandma.

"No way." Carrying the stick and pads and hoisting the canvas hockey bag over my shoulder, I'm ready. "There are rules in our family that keep everything from being too crazy. Mom would be so tired if she carried all of our hockey bags. Besides, it's a hockey tradition. You get laughed at if you don't carry your own bag."

Sometimes when Grandma and Grandpa are here, they help by driving me to my hockey games. Grandpa carries my bag, and Grandma carries my goalie pads and stick. That's special.

"It's as close to being an athlete as I get," Grandma will say. She likes to laugh at her little joke.

"Ready, Caley?" asks Dad at the door.

"Score goals, Caley!" Grandma and Grandpa yell as Dad and I leave for my first game as a forward. They're babysitting Tara tonight.

"I'm not home much, so I can't wait to see you play," says Dad.

"Does that mean I'm carrying my own bag again?" I ask.

"A good hockey player always carries her own equipment." He grins. So, I carry my own bag. Besides, my brothers give me a hard time if I don't. I can't let that happen. We're pretty competitive. I like sharing hockey with the rest of my family. My dad is really encouraging and proud of me. My whole family is, but my brothers won't admit it—ever.

"Dad, Coach says I could be a forward tonight. Maybe I'll score. Coach says if we win, we'll go to a tournament in Cincinnati—our first one."

Dad smiles and says, "Go for it, Caley. But you'll have to work hard."

That's another one of his favorite sayings. I feel relieved he doesn't sound disappointed that I'm not the goalie. I didn't mention the part about talking to Coach. Maybe I'll tell him tomorrow.

In the locker room there's lots of talking, laughing, and just plain nervous energy flying everywhere.

"I heard you're not our goalie tonight. We better be careful. Play good defense!" says Madison.

"Everyone has heard we might go to a tournament. We have to win every game." announces Emily.

"Alex, I can't wait for the game to start. I know I'll score tonight." She gives me her thumbs-up.

"My dad is here. I bet he'll be happy if I score," I say.

"We'll all be happy if you score."

"I'll probably get a goal," says Emily. "You haven't been a forward, Caley. You need practice."

"Don't worry, I'll score," I say, trying to sound positive.

Emily has good hands and is an aggressive player. She thinks she's the best scorer on our team. Well, maybe she is.

I'll show her, I think. *She's working hard to prove she can do it even if she's small.*

Both teams are on the ice, warming up before the game. As we're skating around the rink, I'm glad I'm not the goalie and Janie is. She's a good, average player in any position and always positive about everything.

I'm feeling sorry for her as she skates awkwardly around the ice with all that goalie equipment on. It's hard to stay limber when you're just standing around inside a net.

I'm so glad it's not me.

CHAPTER 6

We are waiting for the game to start. Coach yells, "All right, first line, let's go."

My heart pounds. I'm the first one back on the ice. We all yell, "Go Rangers!" and take our positions.

The game begins. The referee drops the puck. We all scramble for it. The other team wins the puck and charges down the ice. The rest of us race after them.

I love the game of ice hockey. Skating as fast as I can to catch up with the player from the other team is fun. Taking the puck away with my stick and racing toward the net is really fun. It usually ends in a scramble as somebody tries to get a shot—whack, the sound of the stick hitting the puck!

Sometimes the puck goes wide of the net, sometimes it goes nowhere, and sometimes the other team gets it and we're off to the other end of the ice. There's always movement, our long hair flying from under our helmets, the team members all taking care of each other. That's another good part. Sometimes we stop to help a player who has fallen down. My brothers would never do that when they're on the ice. Coach doesn't think it's a good idea either, especially during a game. I think that girls' hockey must be nicer than boys' hockey.

I mumble to myself a lot as I race around: "Remember to stay

focused. Move with the team, up and down the ice. Try and stay in position. Keep your eye on the puck, your teammates, the other team. Don't trip over anyone who's down on the ice. Don't trip over your own feet—that's embarrassing."

By the beginning of the third and last period, we're ahead by a score of three to one. I still haven't had a shot at the net, but I keep trying. Suddenly a player from the other team is right in front of me with the puck. Skating hard, I get close to her. Leaning closer, she's distracted and loses control. I take it away and start down the ice. *Keep it going. Keep it going.*

I lose it. Alex picks it up and keeps going.

"Take it down, Caley," she yells, and she passes the puck back.

She's giving me the chance to score. I have the puck. I'm so excited I can hardly breathe. It looks clear.

I take a shot as hard as I can. It seems to take forever. And then, at last, it slides between the skates of the other team's goalie and right into their net.

The whistle blows. The referee signals. Goal!

"I scored a goal!" I yell. I throw my arms up, jumping up and down on my skates. It's so exciting that I can't stand it. The crowd cheers. I flop on the ice, lying on my back with my feet in the air, arms outstretched, hockey stick clutched in my hand. I don't know what to do with myself. I'm so happy.

My goal is the last of the game. The Rangers win.

"Good job!" says Alex in the locker room. "I think the coach will let you be a forward now."

"We did it, didn't we? Thanks for that perfect pass."

"We're going to be in a tournament. We're real hockey players," Alex says.

"I scored! I scored!" I jump up and down and give everybody high fives.

Emily walks up to me and says, "Think you're smart, don't you? So you scored—big deal. It wasn't the winning goal. I got that."

I step closer to her and give her the look. I don't know what it is, but it works on my family (well, sometimes). It's something like being mad and scolding without words. That's how it feels to me anyway. I don't know where it comes from, but I've always had it.

I lock eyes with Emily until she finally looks away and leaves. I don't think she'll give me a hard time again. It must have been a good, ferocious look.

"Emily is really feisty," says Alex. "Being the youngest and smallest on our team, I guess she has to be."

"She pumps her legs up and down the ice, trying to keep up. It's fun to watch her. She's a tough, hard player," I say.

"Alex, I can't wait to tell the rest of the family about my goal. I've heard my brothers' goal-scoring stories fifty times. I think they've been playing hockey since they could walk. That's a lot of old stories to listen to. Now I have a story too."

"Some big brothers like to act important," says Alex. "But yours are kind of cute. I like them."

"They're weird, Alex. You must be kidding."

"You just think that because they're your brothers, Caley. I'd love to have a big brother. You're lucky that you have two. Besides they're so cool. I only have little brothers. They're a pain."

"Well, some days they're okay, sort of. Like Dean helped me practice this week. And your little brothers are sweet," I say.

"Your brother Jake is my favorite. I love his big brown eyes." Alex sighs. "So cute."

I'm groaning, rolling my eyes at her and laughing as we leave the building.

When Dad and I get home, everyone is there. They all gather around the kitchen table to hear about the game.

I can tell by the smell in the house that my brothers were in the garage, working on forming the perfect curve in their hockey sticks. They use a special kind of blowtorch thing. It smells like something awful burning, maybe their socks. I'm surprised they stopped to hear about the game.

"Tell us what happened, Caley," says Mom.

"Yea, tell us what happened," the others say.

"Who won?"

"Were you a forward?"

"Did you score?"

"Did you get to play, or did you have to sit on the bench the whole time?" asks Jake.

"Yes, I played. I even scored a goal."

"I loved it," Dad says, "when you threw your arms up over your head after you scored. But lying on the ice with your feet in the air may have been pushing it a little."

"It was exciting. And now we're going to our first tournament," I say.

My brothers are surprised. I can tell because for once they don't say anything—not even a snort.

CHAPTER 7

The next week after practice, Coach calls a short meeting. "Good job, girls. You learned the basic rules of hockey in only a few months. Even more important, you apply them. You've won every game. After last week's win, we clinched a spot in the tournament in Cincinnati.

"The tournament," he explains, "will last four days. A team gets points for every win and points for every tie. If we lose three games, we're out of the tournament. So, we will be playing three to six games. When the points are added up, the two teams with the most points will play for the championship. We have a lot more games to play before we leave. If you work hard and keep winning, we'll be ready by tournament time."

"Also," he adds, "as usual, parents who can drive will take anyone who needs a ride. So, start making your plans now. I'll have more information later on. There will be handouts with maps and places to stay," he says, leaving the locker room.

"Wow," says Alex, "this will really be a trip."

"Our first tournament. Who do you think we'll be playing? Do you think they're good, better than we are?"

"Who knows? I guess that's why they have tournaments," Alex says.

"Coach never tells us much ahead of time," I say.

"You're beginning to worry already."

"Winning our first tournament would be sweet."

"Just going to another city will be fun," Alex says.

"My mom says if we go to tournament, she'll drive. Cincinnati is a long way, at least four hours. If your parents can't go, you can ride with us. Our van is big. It holds a lot of hockey equipment. Tara is going and any team member who needs a ride. We'll take as many as we have room for," I say.

"I don't think my parents will be able to go because of my new baby sister. I'll ask my mom to call your mom. They can work it out. It'll be fun to go together."

The next few games are great. Everyone works harder because they know the tournament is coming. We act more like a team, and we win every game.

I get scoring chances and even score some goals. I love scoring goals. It's great being a forward, and playing center is cool.

Coach is rotating goaltenders, and everyone seems happy, especially me. Sometimes at practice he asks me to help out the goalies on little things, like how to handle the awkward goalie stick. Keeping your balance in a crouched position while you try to stop a puck with that big stick can be tricky.

"Just keep your feet well planted," I tell them. "It's hard to do on slippery ice with skates on. I know; I've fallen down a lot."

After one of our practices, I see Coach by himself and skate over.

"Thanks for letting me play forward instead of goaltending. I'm having fun," I say.

He smiles and says, "I'm glad you're happy. That's what playing sports is all about: having fun."

I know that playing hockey as you get older is more than fun. My dad still loves playing hockey, but no coach ever tells him or his team to have fun. They'd probably laugh at him. The game at that level is tough.

CHAPTER 8

Finally, the big day we've been waiting for arrives. It's early in the morning on the first day of the tournament. Parents drop off some of my teammates at my house. Alex, Janie, and Madison are going with us. We pack the van with hockey equipment, suitcases, and snacks like trail mix, Gatorade, and my favorite: chocolate cupcakes with white frosting. You need energy for a long drive.

"Mom, it's starting to snow. Are you okay driving in this?" I ask.

"It's really snowing hard," says Alex after we finally get started.

Mom drives slowly.

"It's hard to see with the wind blowing the snow across the highway," she says.

"It feels like we're just inching along the road," I say. "What if we're late for the first game?"

"Stop worrying, Caley," Janie says. "We'll be fine."

"It's taking forever. When does this snow stop?"

Some of our excitement wears off. Everyone sits quietly, playing with Gameboys, watching videos, or snoozing.

I can hear Tara and Alex playing gin rummy, Tara's favorite card game. I wonder how long it will take Alex to figure out why Tara always wins. I grin to myself.

Tara is eight years old and can play "Let's Pretend" for hours.

Someday she'll write a Broadway play or the funniest movie ever. I think she's bored with hockey, but she's a trooper. She hangs in there with us and doesn't complain much. Mostly, Tara just wants a dog. She never stops talking about the dog she wishes she had. She even has a doghouse in her bedroom—but no dog. Sometimes I get tired of hearing about that dog.

It's boring sitting in the van. I just want to get there.

At last, Mom says, "We're almost there. Start getting your things together. You'd better hurry. We'll make it just in time for the first game."

"Whew, that was a long drive."

Mom pulls up in front of the rink. The van empties fast. We haul hockey bags, sticks, and pads into the building.

This arena has five youth rinks. It smells like all hockey rinks: like hot dogs, sweat, and popcorn. The lobby usually feels cold, but I never think the ice does. I don't know why. The areas around every rink are always crowded with kids coming and going. There are video games, snack bars, and small shops selling hockey equipment, in case you forget something.

Some of the team and their families are waiting by the door, clapping, cheering, and yelling, "You made it!"

They point toward the locker room we will be using.

"We worried you wouldn't get here in time," shouts someone. "We'd have to forfeit."

Ignoring them, we rush to get suited up.

"No time to be nervous, Alex. Let's go. Isn't it exciting? The first game of our first tournament."

"I'm not nervous," she says, "but I think you are."

"Just excited," I say.

"Caley," she whispers, "I heard the first team we're playing isn't very good."

"Do you think we'll win this one?" I ask.

When we are all seated on the bench, Coach comes over and says, "I want you to remember the things you've learned and practiced together. You can beat this team. Janie will be our goalie for our first game. Now have fun."

A sigh of relief—it's not me.

My heart beats faster. It's exciting. I can't wait for the game to begin.

Finally, we form a circle on the ice, bending over, heads together, holding hands. With a shout of "Go Rangers" and a whoop, we're off and in position.

The whistle blows. The referee drops the puck.

The first game of our first tournament begins.

The first line is on the ice. We have three lines on our team. Each one has five players, offense and defense. The lines take turns. Coach usually signals when to switch, usually after thirty or forty-five seconds. That's the rule, so we don't get tired. Sometimes it depends on what's happening on the ice. I'm not quite sure of that yet. We just do what he says, but sometimes he forgets.

After the first ten-minute period, I whisper to Alex, "You were right. This team isn't very good. We can do this."

The second and third periods pass quickly, and the game is over. We win five to zero. Madison, Emily, and Alex scored. I got two assists. We all feel good.

Coach gathers us around the bench and says, "I know you've had a long traveling day, so get a good night's sleep. You did a nice job. You played well. See you for a meeting before practice tomorrow. We'll talk about the next team we're playing. I know you're all going out for pizza, so have fun."

51

"It's a good start to the tournament, Alex. Isn't it a relief to get the first game over?" I say.

"That team was easy," she says. "I hope they're all like that."

The locker room is loud with laughing, shouts, and high fives. We are hyped. The first game of our first tournament is behind us.

A shout is heard. "Time for pizza!"

Parents and kids all rush to the restaurant. We sit and talk nonstop about hockey, in between mouthfuls of pizza—lots of pizza.

CHAPTER 9

"Good job goaltending, Janie. They didn't score, not even one goal."

Maybe she'll be the goaltender every time, I think. *I don't need to worry. But that's not fair for Janie, unless she wants to be.*

"You didn't score today, Caley," says Emily. She sounds pleased.

It's not long before parents gather everyone for bed.

"What a fun day. Goodnight, everybody. See you at breakfast," I say.

The next morning while practicing before the game, Coach calls his meeting.

"This team will be harder to beat," he says. "Play as well as you did yesterday, and you won't have any trouble. Madison will be our goalie."

He shares what he knows about the other team, talking about strategy and ways we can win the game.

"Remember the importance of defense. Visualize what you will do in different situations," he says. "Most of all, have fun."

Madison wrinkles up her nose. I guess she doesn't like goaltending either. What a relief it's not me. I keep hoping my turn doesn't come up. Maybe it won't if I can just score goals.

I glance at the stands, which hold about two hundred people. Youth rinks are smaller than regulation rinks. The structures are all different. In this rink the fans, mostly parents and kids, are all sitting in bleachers

on one side. The benches for both teams are across the ice. The penalty boxes are on the same side as the fans. Some dads like to yell advice when you're in the penalty box. Usually it just embarrasses the kids. Some parents yell all the time about everything. When you're on the ice, you usually don't pay attention or even hear them. My dad whistles and then does hand signals. That's usually helpful, but for this tournament, he's traveling on the West Coast and can't be here.

The entire rink is enclosed by "the boards," a fence that helps to keep the puck in. Hockey players like to push each other into the boards. It makes a loud noise and throws the other player off balance. It doesn't hurt, even though it looks like it does.

"I see your mom and Tara standing along the boards," says Alex.

They're smiling. Standing there, they'll get to see everything. "It's fun to have part of my family here. If my brothers were here, they'd have to tell me what they think I'm doing wrong, all the time. Who needs that?" I say.

"It would be fun to have your brothers here," says Alex, and then she grins.

"Right, Alex, you'd love them around, especially Jake. You seem to have a thing for him," I say. "To me, he's just an irritation—always on my case, nagging, teasing, or grumbling about something."

"Never," says Alex. "You're exaggerating. You're mean. He's too cute."

"Oh, brother, I can't wait to tell him you said that."

Coach is yelling: "Game time. First line on the ice."

"That's us. Let's go."

The referee drops the puck. There's a big scramble for it as game two begins.

In the first period we don't score. We were pretty sloppy.

Coach yells, "You are going to have to work a lot harder than that if you want to stay in this tournament!"

He's right.

The ref drops the puck to start the second period. A player from the other team grabs the puck and races toward our net. She's fast. We skate as hard as we can to catch up. Emily falls down. Slowing so we don't trip over her, we keep going. The player from the other team has time to line up a shot. Madison doesn't see it coming. It sails right into our net. They're ahead one to zero. With their sticks in the air, the other team is cheering. Their fans are yelling and stomping their feet. I hate it when that happens.

The whistle blows for the start of the third period.

I watch the referee drop the puck. I want that puck. Everyone is after it. It squishes out toward the edge of the rink, right near me. I have it with my stick. I start up the ice, along the boards. Skating as hard as I can, I am careful not to lose control.

The net gets closer. I take a shot. The puck goes wide. It is picked up by Alex. She passes it back. I jam it at the net and then jam it again. I have to get that puck past their goalie.

It goes in. A goal—I did it!

The score is tied.

The third period is almost over. Suddenly, Emily races down the ice on her little legs and slaps the puck right in. We win our second game by one point. The fans clap and cheer. I didn't know we had so many.

"You worked hard for that win," says Coach in the locker room. "They're a good team, and they didn't make it easy for you. Now I'd suggest you rest up, because you'll be playing again tonight. The game won't start until 8:30 p.m., so we have lots of time. Get something to eat, and relax. I'll talk to you again later."

CHAPTER 10

The locker room is quiet. I dress slowly, feeling tired and relieved. Some teams play up to four games a day. That takes energy.

I wonder what Mom and Tara are doing this afternoon. Sometimes Mom takes us to an aquarium or some other interesting place, but usually most of the team spends time in the pool, playing video games, or practicing with mini sticks in the hospitality room. Mini sticks are small hockey sticks about two feet long. We hit rubber balls into a small net or overturned plastic basket, whatever's handy. That's my favorite pastime. I guess it's supposed to improve our hand-eye coordination, but I think it's just fun.

When we get back to the hotel, I find Tara reading in our room.

"Let's head for the pool, Tara. I feel like a swim before we have to head back to the rink."

"Okay," she says, putting down her book. She loves to read. I wonder if she's bored again. At least she did not bring her dog along.

Most of the team and a few families are at the pool.

"Come on in," someone yells. "We're playing Marco Polo."

"The pool room is all echo-eey," says Madison. "We're not doing very well. Nobody's getting it right."

Our voices bounce off the walls like a big drum. We laugh so hard

that we can hardly stand up in the water. Suddenly, two beach balls are thrown in.

"Forget Marco Polo; let's play volleyball," yells Emily.

"We'll form teams."

"Great idea."

We form two teams. There's a lot of jumping, splashing, and hitting as we try and figure out what we're doing.

"Over here," yells Janie, and everyone rushes in that direction.

"No over here," yells Madison as she gets smacked with a ball. We're all over the pool, making up rules as we go along. The balls are tossed out of the water a lot, bouncing on the walls.

Pretty soon the other people in the pool join in the game. Brothers and sisters, families of all ages are playing. The pool is full of people smashing volleyballs, laughing, and splashing. We manage to have two balls in the air, flying everywhere. Tara is really good at whipping balls at the other team. She's a good volleyball player.

"What's the score?" I ask.

"We don't know, but we must be winning." answers Emily.

"The people sitting around the pool are beginning to look grouchy," says Janie.

"I think we're getting people sitting in the chairs a little wet," I say.

"It's a pool area," says Madison. "It's wet."

"Everyone's leaving," I say.

"Do you think those people will complain to the manager?" asks Alex.

"Maybe," says Madison, "but we'll keep playing. We can't get anyone wet that's not here."

Parents start flagging us down.

"Time to get ready for the game," they say, throwing towels at us.

Someone's mother passes out sandwiches. They are really good. It's nice of her to be thinking of us starving hockey players.

CHAPTER 11

Finally, we're back at the rink again, and we're all ready to go and excited. Out on the ice, Alex is giving everyone, her thumbs-up. Madison is the goalie again. I hope Coach has forgotten about me. Sighing, I'm getting more worried about being called to be the goalie. Actually, everyone's getting tenser as the games go on.

The referee drops the puck, and off we go. We're psyched. We seem to have a little less energy than that morning, but we're working hard. We win our third game two to one.

The next day we hear that some teams are dropping out.

"I think the teams that are left must be pretty good," says Alex.

"I know. They're going to be harder to beat," I say.

A couple of us try to calculate the other teams' points as close as we can, so we know where we stand. Enough teams are still playing that the final numbers won't be in until all the rounds in all the rinks are over.

"How many points do the Flames have?" asks Emily. "I hear they're beating everybody. I want to know more about them."

Emily sounds frustrated, but we're all getting nervous and testy. It's getting harder.

Coach arrives for another meeting and says, "Don't spend too much time worrying about the other teams' points; they change too quickly.

We won't know the playoff standings until the games are almost done. You have nothing to worry about.

"You're really coming together as a team. I'm proud of you," he says. "Just remember to have fun."

"He needs a new speech," says Alex under her breath.

"He didn't answer my question about the Flames," says Emily. "He knows the standings. Does he think I'm dumb? Is he being protective? How stupid is that? Let's find out when they're playing on one of these rinks. We'll watch them and see for ourselves what's happening."

"Watching the Flames play is a good idea, Emily. How do you know about them?" I ask.

"I have friends who have friends that know someone on the Flames team."

We easily win our next game. Is it too easy? We can't get too sure of ourselves. Before I can think that one over, we head for the lobby, stopping people to ask about the Flames. Finding out about their schedule isn't easy.

"Do you know when and where the Flames are playing?" we ask everyone. Finally, a dad tells us he saw them go through the lobby about thirty minutes before.

"They went that way." He points to a rink on the other end of the building.

We walk into the rink he pointed out and hear a noisy crowd. The Flames are ahead and in control. They look mean and tough, pushing and shoving players around.

"They're big," says Emily. "Really big. They must be old."

"That's high sticking," Alex shouts. "The referee didn't even call it. That Flames player should be in the penalty box. She shoved that stick in the other player's face mask."

"Where does this team come from?" Emily demands answers. "They'll kill us."

At last the whistle blows and a Flames player goes to the penalty box for tripping.

"Do you think we could end up playing them?" I ask.

"I think we've seen enough," says Madison. She looks scared.

"See," says Emily, "I told you they were tough. Now will someone listen to me?"

As we head back to the hotel, we don't talk much. We are depressed.

"The Flames are looking hard to beat," I mutter.

"Maybe we won't have to play them," says Madison.

"Hope you're right," I say.

"Why didn't we ask one of those noisy fans how many games they've lost? We haven't lost any. That would give us a clue."

"All we really know is they will be a hard team to beat," I say.

All the excitement of winning our last game is gone.

CHAPTER 12

Today's our fourth game in three days. If we win, we play again tomorrow morning, the last day of the tournament. We're so excited and giddy that we're telling dumb "knock-knock" jokes.

We meet in the hospitality room and Coach says, "Get the mini sticks and baskets. We'll practice shooting."

"These baskets are much smaller than a regular net, so you have to be more accurate," says Emily. She's firing tennis balls one after another into the baskets.

"I must admit, Emily, you're pretty good. Being the youngest and smallest on the team must be hard sometimes. You're fun to practice with," I says.

"Thanks," she says, looking surprised. "You're better at being a forward than I thought you'd be."

"You two have finally figured it out," says Alex.

Alex is great at passing to us, and she's a good scorer too. We take turns passing and shooting.

"Does anyone want to practice being the goalie?" I ask. "We'll shoot pucks at you."

"No," several players yell. "Not us. Shooting at the net is more fun."

We never know who the goalie will be in any game, so we don't

pay much attention. Our goaltenders, usually Janie and Madison, are doing a good job.

"Do you think we'll win this tournament, Alex?" I ask her for the hundredth time.

"We have another game or two to win first," she says. "I know the Flames are good. I hope we won't have to play them. Coach isn't talking."

We win the day's game against a team I've never heard of, by just one point. Both Janie and Emily score. I had an assist on Emily's goal and managed to score a goal as well. Our defense is working hard and getting better every game, but it's getting harder to beat the other teams.

"We still won't know if we'll be in the final playoff game until after our fifth game tomorrow morning," says Alex.

"And we won't know what team we'll be playing if we make it," I add.

"Better not be those Flames," Emily says, shaking her head.

It's the morning of the last day of the tournament, and our fifth game is hard. The other team is ahead most of the time. We just pull it out at the end. Alex assists Emily for a last-minute goal, and the game is over.

We become more nervous. Emily keeps complaining about anything and everything. Alex tries to calm her down, over and over. Madison isn't talking, not a word. She doesn't answer when you speak to her. I'm feeling like I have to giggle all the time. I hope it doesn't show. I have to clamp my hand over my mouth to keep quiet. If I start laughing, I won't be able to stop.

Coach gathers us together in the locker room to announce the standings.

"The team with the second most points is the Flames," he says. "And the team with the most points is you, the Rangers! Congratulations.

You're going to be playing for the championship. The final playoff game will begin at three o'clock this afternoon." He gives us all high-fives and beams with pride. "You have a good chance of winning the championship."

We begin screaming and jumping up and down.

"Alex, it's so exciting, I can hardly stand it," I say.

We settle down a bit, and Coach says there will be a very short practice and meeting before the game that afternoon. He gives us all a salute and leaves the locker room.

"Can you believe it, Alex? We're in the championship game."

We look at each other and say, "The Flames! We're playing the Flames in the final game."

The locker room grows quieter.

"Oh no, not the Flames," someone mutters. "I heard about them. They're good."

"But we're better. We have more points," Alex says.

"You don't really think that helps. Tell it to the Flames in the middle of the game," Emily says. "'You can't win, we have more points.'"

"This will be hard, Alex," I say.

Reality is sinking in. My stomach begins to hurt.

"I don't think I'll have much lunch today. Maybe plain butterfly pasta with broccoli and butter. It's a good thing it's my favorite food. I don't need a stomach ache before the game," I say.

"We all need a carbo load to keep our energy level up," says Alex.

"Why don't some of us get together and work on our passing and scoring with our mini sticks? We're pretty good at it."

"We'll need it for the Flames," says Emily.

"I hope they haven't figured our system out," says Alex. "Has their coach been watching us play?"

"He probably has, or someone's father who helps out. Our coach has

been watching them, I'm sure. They've been talking to each other. They do it all the time," I say. "Don't worry, Alex. We'll score goals and win."

"Lots of goals," says Emily.

Emily and I've switched places with Alex. We're reassuring her for a change.

We drift off to lunch, and before we know it, it's time to go to the rink. Before the game, we gather in the locker room. Coach is there with a big smile.

"Let's get suited up and then do a few rounds on the ice." He gives us some pointers on what to watch for from the other team. "Just a reminder, there has to be a winner. These are the rules for Ten and Under Girls Municipal Recreational League. In case of a tied score, there is a five-minute overtime period. If no one scores in the overtime period, we go into a shootout."

"And then what? Still no score?" Emily asks.

"Then we repeat the shootout," Coach says.

"But we've never been in a shootout," Emily says.

"It won't happen, so don't worry."

"He sounds like he thinks that's another dumb question," says Emily loudly to herself.

We get a calming grin from Coach.

"There seems to be a lot of phony comforting going on here," says Emily under her breath. "I'm worried about those Flames. With them, anything can happen. They're tough and mean."

"He's trying to make it sound easy," I say, getting suited up.

"He looks pretty tense to me," says Emily. "That's not a good sign. I'll bet he doesn't like the Flames either."

"Maybe a shootout's just like mini sticks hockey with an overturned wastebasket," says Alex. Emily and I roll our eyes at her.

"Right, Alex," says Emily. "We'll keep that in mind."

CHAPTER 13

"Have you noticed that the bleachers are full of people?" says Madison. "There's not even standing room by the boards. I thought some teams had gone home. They must be staying to watch the final game. This is scary."

"I know hockey players like to watch Detroit play, because the city has such good teams."

"Do you think they're here to see us?" says Emily.

"Who knows?" Alex says as she begins a warm-up trip around the rink.

I put on my skates and start down the ice toward Mom and Tara, who are at the boards. Tara always has smiles, especially in her big brown eyes—my favorite cheerleader. Skating up, I wave for good luck.

Coach skates toward me on the ice. He yells, "Caley, stop a minute. I want to talk to you."

"Me?"

"Caley, I want you to be the goaltender for this championship game. You're our best chance of winning."

My mouth falls open—oh no, the goaltender in the championship game. I stare at him. *Did I hear right?*

"It has to be your decision," he says.

Goaltender in the final playoff game. I don't want to be the goalie. It's too scary. What if I blow it? I don't know what to do.

"It's for the team," adds Coach.

I turn to Mom and Tara, who are standing nearby.

"Coach wants me to be the goaltender in this game. I don't know what to do. I'm so nervous," I whisper to Mom. "What if we lose, and it's my fault?"

"Caley," she says, "Coach wouldn't have asked you if he didn't think you could do it."

But she looks worried too.

"Wow," says Tara quietly. Her big brown eyes are even larger.

"It will be the hardest thing I've ever done," I say. *We have to win. I have to make a decision.*

My teammates are all on the ice, patiently watching and waiting. They're looking at me and seem to be hoping. My team—I can't let them down.

Finally, I look at Coach and say, "Okay, I'll be the goalie. For the team."

"Are you sure?" Coach asks. "I know you don't like being a goalie."

The tone in his voice tells me he's already decided. I nod my head yes, but I'm not sure at all.

"Better hurry and get suited up," he says.

Sighing, I skate back to the bench. The pile of goaltending equipment is waiting for me.

How did this happen? I think. Suddenly I know it wasn't my decision at all.

"Emily, why didn't I notice that coach hadn't assigned anyone to be the goalie?" I ask.

"I'm glad it's not me," she says happily. "Just don't let them run you over in the net. That can hurt."

The game is about to start, and I still need to put all my stuff on. I have shin guards under my stockings, which attach to my blue uniform shorts with Velcro. Over the shin guards and stockings go the big, heavily padded leg guards. They attach to my skates, extend above my knees, and tie behind my legs.

"Sometimes I'm glad I'm little," says Emily, helping with one of the leg guards. "This equipment is so big and heavy that I practically fall down. I think Coach feels sorry for me. I feel like a clunky robot with all that stuff on. It's too hard for me to move around in the net."

For a minute I think that maybe Emily has wanted to be a goalie but can't because she's so small.

She hands me the chest protector. Attached to the chest protector are shoulder pads and elbow pads. The chest protector ties behind my back. Alex and a few other teammates skate over and help me adjust it.

"I'm glad you're going to be the goalie for us," Alex says. "You'll do a great job. I know you will."

"I guess our pass and shoot practice won't be of much use now, Alex, but you and Emily can do it. Janie and Madison will help," I say. I can't talk anymore. I'm so scared.

Alex hands me the neck guard and then the mouth guard. I pick up the caged helmet, the gridlike face mask and helmet that's all in one piece, and shove it over my long hair. Finally, I put on the long, padded gloves. Picking up the wide goalie stick, I just have time to skate around the rink. It helps me get adjusted to the weight of the equipment.

Adult goalie equipment weighs forty pounds. This weighs at least twenty-five pounds, but it feels heavier right now because I haven't worn it in a while. It feels like it weighs half as much as I do.

As I get back to the bench, Coach comes over to check the pads and makes some adjustments. "Move around, Caley, and see how it feels. Are you comfortable?"

I nod. My mind is already on the game. I have to stop pucks. If I don't, we lose.

Skating to the Rangers net, I hit on both sides of the metal frame. It's called banging the pipes and is supposed to bring good luck. It also helps me feel the size of the space I have to defend. A few stretches and I settle into position, knees slightly bent. I remember the advice about goaltending that Dad gave me a few months ago, when I was always the goalie. He said, "Look big, like this." I try to visualize how he stood: knees bent, feet firmly apart, in a crouch. He also said to remember to keep my elbows in for better stick control. That's easier.

I let out a deep breath.

Alex flashes me her thumbs-up from the bench. I wobble my goalie stick back at her.

The first line comes out and gets in position. The whistle blows. The ref drops the puck. The championship game begins.

And I'm the goaltender.

CHAPTER 14

Both teams race up and down the ice. Alex gets the puck and passes to Emily. A Flames player intercepts the pass and play starts in my direction. Our defense pokes at the puck and sends it off to the boards. Now the action heads toward the other net. My eyes never leave the play and the puck.

I feel my hands getting sweaty. My throat is dry. I'm glad I have a bottle of water lying on top of the cage, if there is time to drink it.

Emily gets the puck. She sends it to the other net. It goes wide. I have one eye on the clock, counting down the minutes left in the first period. Suddenly, a Flames player is out in front. She has good control of the puck. She heads straight for my net.

My elbows are in, and my stick is in position. The puck heads into the net. I can't reach it. It slides right past my left foot. I miss. The Flames score!

Flames fans clap and cheer. Rangers fans boo. I hear the hockey dads standing behind me, moaning and groaning. I watch as they throw up their hands and turn their backs. They walk away.

I feel the tears running down my cheeks. I can't wipe them away because of my face mask and heavy gloves. My heart hurts. My stomach aches.

I look over at Mom standing along the boards. I know she sees the

tears. She looks so sad—and worried. I know she feels bad for me. Tara's mouth is open. She's standing still like a statue, staring.

I'm letting everybody down.

The tears are drying on my face when the whistle blows. Play starts again. There is no time for me to think, which is good.

Up on the electronic scoreboard, the clock shows three minutes left in the first period. The score is one to zero, Flames.

Focus, I think. *This isn't over. Elbows in.*

There's a lot of scrambling on the ice. The teams fight for control of the puck. The Flames get it, and one of their players heads toward my net. The puck dribbles toward me. I stop it with my stick and slap it out to Janie, who is now coming up on the side of the net, yelling, "Over here." She move it back down the ice. I take a deep breath and blow it out.

The buzzer sounds. The clock has run out. The period is over.

We gather the bench during the short break between periods. Somebody passes out water and juice.

Coach says, "That kind of shot is hard to stop, Caley. You're doing a good job. Keep it up."

I notice he doesn't say, "Have fun." That would be annoying.

I get a few taps of encouragement on the head as the first line returns to the ice. Alex gives me a thumbs-up and a big grin. I crouch back in the net. The whistle blows. The second period starts. The clock shows ten minutes and running. Elbows in.

Both teams seem a little slower this period. The big initial rush is wearing off. The Flames are pushing a lot and shoving into the boards. So far there hasn't been much high sticking or tripping. Maybe they figured out you don't win games sitting in the penalty box.

Alex and Emily work on their passing routine, but it's not going well. They have two shots on goal, and both go wide. As the puck hits

the boards, a Flames player grabs it and passes to a teammate. The pass is too hard. No one picks it up. The clock keeps running as both teams regroup.

A player on the other team gets the puck and moves down the ice toward me. As she closes in, our Rangers defense forces her to lose it. They all start back toward the blue line in the center of the rink.

"Yea, defense," I mutter. That was close.

No one on my team seems to be able to get the puck in the net, but it feels like the other team is struggling as much as we are. Both teams fight over the puck for what seems a long time and don't get anywhere. The buzzer sounds the end of the second period. Everyone seems tense.

The goal I missed hangs over my head. I can't miss another shot. We skate over to the bench.

"The way you score goals is to keep trying. You'll miss the net a lot, but sooner or later the puck will go in. This period you'll score," says Coach. "Now get out there and get to work. Second line on the ice."

Back in my net, I bang the pipes for good luck and get in position.

"Come on, Rangers. You have to score." I say out loud to myself. "I can't let the Flames score."

The puck drops for the face off. The third period is underway. After a scramble, someone whacks the puck against the boards. Emily takes it down the ice and shoots. She misses. One of the Flames grabs it and brings it back up the ice. She heads my way. As she nears my net, she begins to lose control of the puck. Her shot is sloppy. It's easy to stop. I drop to my knees and cover it with both gloves, not taking any chances.

The crowd roars and cheers, "Good save!" I feel better now.

Again, the face off and the puck is pushed, shoved, and whacked around. The other team works to keep us from scoring. We try hard to score. Alex and Emily do their play, but it doesn't work

The lines come on and off the ice. Glancing at the clock, I'm

surprised to see only two minutes left. Time is running out. All the Flames have to do is keep us from scoring, and they've won the game.

Suddenly Alex passes the puck to Emily. They race down the ice together, and Emily yells, "Heads up" to Alex. As she nears the net, Alex takes a shot, and the goalie stops it. Emily gets the rebound. The puck goes in. She scores!

The crowd yells and claps. The players on the bench bang sticks against the boards. The whistle blows. There's time for a face-off and a scramble for the puck. The buzzer sounds. The game ends. It's a one-to-one tie!

We all go to the bench. Finally, I can take off my heavy gloves and give Alex a thumbs-up with my sweaty hand.

"Good job, Alex." Everyone raps on her helmet. There is a feeling of relief that we're still in the game. We haven't lost yet.

Coach calls for our attention and says, "As you know, there has to be a winner when you play for the championship. In one minute, we will go into a five-minute overtime. If no one scores, there will be a shootout. I'll explain that later if I need to."

"I hate when he does that. Does he think we're stupid?" asks Emily. "Does he think we can't handle knowing about a dumb shootout?"

"We know about shootouts, Emily," says Alex.

"But we've never been in one," she says.

"He always does that, Emily. Don't worry about it now. We have to win in this overtime." Alex is reassuring again, calming Emily down.

"Check your equipment and get ready," yells Coach.

It felt good to get my face mask and helmet off for a minute. My hair is all sweaty and sticking to my head. I try to shake it to cool down.

Coach comes over and asks, "How are you, Caley? Are you ready?" He checks and adjusts the back of my chest protector and knee pads and helps put my face mask, helmet, and gloves back on.

"It looks like you're good to go, Caley. Good luck."

I travel back to the net. I bang the pipes, get into a crouch, and position the stick, trying to remember how Dad looked when he said to "Look big." I imagine he meant taking up all the space in the net. Nothing can get by me—I hope. Breathe.

I can't believe we're going into overtime. Now, I'm really nervous, sweaty, and scared. Only five minutes and it will be over—a long five minutes.

The whistle blows. The puck drops. Overtime begins. The clock runs. Players on both teams try hard. There's a lot of passing, but the receivers aren't there. Skaters collide and sprawl on the ice. All the action is in the middle of the ice between the blue lines. I watch carefully.

And then it happens.

A Flames player breaks free and skates along the boards with the puck—right toward me. I'm ready, watching and tense. She slaps the puck at the net. It bounces off the pipe. Using my stick, I move out and deflect it. I yell, "Get it, Madison," as she's picks it up and starts skating back down the ice.

The crowd roars. The clock still runs. Finally, Courtney has the puck and heads toward the net. She is intercepted by a Flames player. Emily gets the puck back and passes to Alex. She shoots. It goes wide, and there is a loud moan from the crowd.

The scoreboard still shows a one-to-one tie. The seconds run down. My team tries hard, but they haven't been able to score. The buzzer sounds. Overtime ends. Nobody scored.

We gather once more at the bench. We all look tired. It's quiet.

"Listen up," says Coach. "We're going into a shootout."

"I knew it," says Emily. "Why doesn't he listen to me?"

Coach continues, saying, "That means that five players on each side will take turns, alternating, trying to shoot the puck into the net.

Whoever scores the most goals will win. Are there any questions? Emily, Alex, Madison, Courtney, and Janie will represent our team."

"Are we having fun yet?" says Emily, skating away.

She makes me laugh. I sound weird. *Get a grip. Don't fall apart now,* I think. *Headline: Goalie collapses in hysterics. She won't stop giggling.*

Coach comes over to where I'm standing. "Are you ready?" he asks.

Gasping and choking, trying to get serious, I nod. I take a deep breath and straighten my shoulders. I can do this.

"You're doing a great job, Caley," he says. "Keep it up, and you'll be fine."

I hardly hear him. I give Alex a thumbs-up and get taps on my helmet for good luck from everyone on the team.

In a shootout the pressure is really on the goalie, because the defense can't help. I feel my heart pounding. My mouth is dry, my hands are sweaty, and my hair is stuck to my head. I skate around the rink to limber up and maybe relax a little.

Alex, Emily, Madison, Courtney, and Janie stand together on the ice, getting ready for their turns in the shootout. The team gathers in a circle and chants, "Let's go, Rangers !" I give each of the five shooters a light punch on the arm. They tap me on the helmet.

"Good luck, you guys. Put every shot in the net," I say.

"We're not worried. You'll save us," says Alex.

"Right."

I skate past Mom and Tara and slow down for another quick wave and more luck.

"Caley!" Tara shouts loudly, with great importance and urgency. "Dad called from California. He wanted to know how the game is going. He can't believe you're the goalie in a shootout. He told Mom to stop you because it's so stressful. You're too young. She told him it's too

late; you're already doing it. He says to tell you he wishes he were here to help. He's just being protective."

It is probably a good thing he's not here. It would be humiliating to be pulled from the game by my dad because it's too stressful. I know he would never quit. Secretly, I know he would never pull me from the game either.

"Thanks, Tara, but there isn't much that helps a goalie in a shootout. Maybe some luck."

"You'll be fine, Caley," Mom says, reassuringly.

"Yes, you'll be wonderful," says Tara.

"I'm not quitting. I'll never quit." I stamp my foot and head straight for my net.

CHAPTER 15

Back in my position, I once again hit the pipes, adjust my mask, go into a crouch, and "look big."

"Here we go again. Am I ready?" No one's there to answer.

The people in the crowd are so quiet, and it's weird. They must be nervous too. I ignore them.

My five teammates chosen to take shots at the net sit on the ice, waiting for their turn. The rest of the team is on the bench. I cross my fingers for the five shooters.

The whistle blows. The first player on my team, Janie, lines up the puck in the center between the blue lines. She starts down the ice toward the Flames's net. She takes a shot and misses. A player from the other team lines up. She skates toward me. The puck dribbles right toward my net. I stop it. The Rangers hockey dads and moms all cheer.

Alex takes the puck down the ice. She pokes it right into the net, under the right foot of their goalie. Score!

I take a deep breath. The next puck comes my way; it goes right into the net. The score in the shootout out is one to one.

The crowd groans again. They're getting a lot noisier.

Courtney takes the puck down the ice. She wings it right into the net. I almost collapse with relief, but then another puck comes my way.

I focus everything on stopping the puck—and I do! Now the score is two to one.

Madison, the fourth shooter for our team, winds up and hits a hard shot. It misses wide. The fourth player from the other team lines up. She hits a slap shot right past my left foot. The score is tied again.

The fifth and last players get ready for the last shot. Emily takes the puck down the ice. She skates toward the right side of the other team's net. As their goalie moves to face her, Emily stops quickly and flips the puck into the left side of their net. The Rangers score!

The crowd goes nuts. They're so loud that I can't hear anything else.

"Ignore them. Don't think about them," I mutter to myself.

The score is three to two in our favor. One last shot by the other team and it will be over—just one more puck for me to stop.

The player lines up the puck. She starts down the ice.

I watch, waiting for her to make her move. She slaps the puck hard. It comes straight at me.

It's not going wide, I think. *It's getting near the net. I have to stop it. I have to give it everything I've got. It's coming closer. Focus, focus, focus. Don't take your eyes off that puck. Be ready. Be ready. Be ready.*

I throw myself down on top of the puck, a big belly-flop flat out on the ice.

Lying on my stomach on the ice, I hear the whistle blow. I search for the puck. I find it under my chest protector and raise it in the air. It didn't go in the net!

We win!

The crowd cheers and yells. My team bangs sticks loudly against the boards. I can hear dads yelling, "Holy moly, what a goalie!"

I struggle to get up with the heavy equipment on and turn toward the bench. It's over.

"Way to go, Caley! We did it!" the team shouts as they rush in my

direction. I'm surrounded by the greatest team in the whole world. They scream as they "jump the goalie." My team is on top of me, and we hit the ice. We're a big, round, happy pile of skates, helmets, and blue and red uniforms. I'm at the bottom of the pile. We're all yelling and hugging whatever part of somebody we can find.

Slowly we untangle. Coach calls for attention. He uses a bullhorn in order to be heard over the crowd.

"Where'd he get that thing?" Emily's asks.

"I have an announcement," he says. "I'd like to present the winning trophy to the Rangers! This is your first tournament, and you won the championship. It is one of the hardest games a hockey player ever has to play—but you won. You did a great job. Congratulations!"

He holds up a large trophy with girl hockey players on it. We clap and cheer, arms and sticks high in the air, and then pound the boards. Parents stomp their feet on the bleachers.

"I have one more important announcement. Listen up." Coach waits for the crowd to settle down.

"Caley didn't want to be the goaltender in our championship game, but she agreed to do it for the team. She worked hard and did a superb job. For being an outstanding team player and a great goalie, today we award Caley the MVP, the most valuable player award."

Surprised, I stand there. Everyone claps and cheers.

I can't believe it—MVP!

"In addition, the entire team and coaching staff would like to present Caley with the winning puck," Coach says.

My team bangs sticks on the ice and boards. Fans cheer. Once more I hear the crowd shouting, "Holy moly, what a goalie!"

Coach skates over and hands me the MVP trophy, and then he gives me the puck. I hold it in the air. Everyone cheers. What a feeling!

My smile must be around my whole head. I can see Mom and Tara beaming.

Both teams line up to shake hands. Everyone grins, but the Rangers' grins are bigger. The Flames form a semicircle and salute us by pounding their sticks three times on the ice and skate off the rink.

"They're cool," says Emily.

I look at my puck as we slowly leave the ice. It feels good. Alex looks over, smiling, and gives me a thumbs-up.

Printed in the United States
By Bookmasters